What Makes School Great?
FRIENDS!

Activities to Build Autism Awareness
and Develop Friendships

Kandis Lighthall, M.A.

Autism and Behavior Training Associates

"Helping you find the keys to
unlock the potential of students
on the Autism Spectrum"

ABTA Publications
Redding, CA, USA

Autism & Behavior Training Associates
ABTA Products and Publications
PO Box 492123
Redding, CA 96049

For information on ordering this manual or on workshops provided by Autism & Behavior Training Associates on this and other topics, please see our websites at:

www.autismandbehavior.com

www.abtaproducts.com

What Makes School Great? FRIENDS!

ISBN: 978-0-9761517-1-5

© 2006 Kandis Lighthall. All rights reserved.
Revised © 2008 Kandis Lighthall. All rights reserved

Permission is hereby granted to photocopy in limited quantities any forms in this publication for the purchaser's instructional use ONLY.
Any commercial use, or use in other publication, regardless of purpose, is prohibited without the author's written permission.

Cover design by Matthew Brinner
Cover photo by James Mazzotta

Printed in U.S.A.

Book manufacturing services provided by
RedTail Book Manufacturing
www.redtail.com

SUSTAINABLE FORESTRY INITIATIVE FIBER USED IN THIS PRODUCT SUPPLIED BY A PARTICIPATING MANUFACTURER AND MEETS THE SOURCING REQUIREMENTS OF THE SFI PROGRAM. WWW.ABOUTSFI.ORG

TABLE OF CONTENTS

Dedication	iv
Preface	v
Introduction	vii
Chapter 1	
Getting Started	1
Chapter 2	
Basic Steps for Awareness Activity	13
Chapter 3	
Variations of Awareness Activities	21
Preschool	21
Kindergarten	22
1st – 2nd Grades	24
3rd – 5th Grades Disability Specific	26
6th – 12th Grades	29
Problem Behaviors Across the Age Groups	31
Chapter 4	
Case Studies	33
High Functioning Autism	33
Classic Autistic Disorder/Non-verbal	36
Asperger Syndrome	38
References	41
Resources on Ability Awareness	42
Books for Young to Elementary Age Children	42
Books for Upper Elementary to Adolescences	43
Books for Adults	44
Books for Self-Awareness	45
Websites for Children and Adults	46
DVD's and Videos	46
Appendix	
A. Ideas for Adults to Create an Awareness Book	47
B. Ideas for Children to Write an Awareness Book	48
C. Planning Form (FOLD OUT)	49

DEDICATION

This manual is dedicated to all the students who have taught me the one thing that always makes school great is having a FRIEND.

And to my father Vincent K. Lundstrom, who at age 88 began to compile his thoughts for a book on a topic that he felt made the greatest difference in his long life. That topic was friends. Although he did not live long enough to finish his book, the great wisdom of his insight is shared though the activities in this manual.

Kandis Lighthall

PREFACE

During my career as a Program Specialist for Autism, I interacted daily with educators who were trying to meet the academic needs of all the students in their classroom, as well as the new set of social challenges the students with ASD presented. The students with ASD struggled to understand the complex and subtle social demands and interactions that bombard them from the minute they arrive on campus until they arrive at home. Their misinterpretation of social situations often prompted the student with ASD to make an unconventional or unexpected response to a peer or teacher. The unconventional response left everyone involved confused and oftentimes frustrated. This situation usually resulted in a call to me to help clear up the confusion, reduce the frustration, and basically make school great again for everyone. This was a "tall order."

I recognized the need to build a shared understanding of the things that make school great for each student. I had led many disability awareness activities in my career; however I decided that I needed to focus on abilities and how we are all more similar than we are different. I also knew that the one thing that usually always makes any situation great is having a friend. With these ideas in mind I developed the ability awareness activity called, What Makes School Great? FRIENDS!

I would like to acknowledge my colleagues, Patricia Schetter, who encouraged me to write this manual and Lauren Bishop who has used the activities and given me great feedback. It is my hope that the manual, What Makes School Great? FRIENDS!, and the variations on this ability awareness theme will give the reader a positive starting point from which to develop greater understanding and deeper relationships for all who participate in the activities.

INTRODUCTION

The number of children identified with an Autism Spectrum Disorder (ASD) has dramatically increased at an alarming rate over the last decade. As the number of students with ASD continues to increase, the public schools have seen more students with these unique needs enter their classrooms. The level of support required to meet the needs of students with ASD is typically addressed through the Individual Education Plan (IEP) process. Even with a well developed IEP, professionals may still feel overwhelmed when trying to meet the student's needs consistently throughout the day. This is especially true in the area of social interaction.

The professional's concern is valid because social demands happen everywhere there are people, and students with ASD will need some degree of support to handle these ever changing social demands. By turning to the research, professionals will discover a solution to their dilemma of meeting daily social needs. The research reveals that there is a large body of human resources that is accessible at every school and can provide consistent daily support, especially in the area of socialization. Thus, we find the solution to our dilemma in this largely untapped human resource, the typical peer group. This group of human resources can be utilized with any age group from preschool through college. Ozonoff, Rogers, and Hendren (2003) report that peer mediated intervention for improving social behavior has produced the largest body of published work. The research has shown that untrained but motivated typical peers may make a difference in the life of a student with ASD or other disability. The studies also reveal that when the typical peer has had some awareness training the outcomes for the student with disabilities can be even greater.

The National Research Council noted in Educating Children with Autism (2001) that, "In the peer-mediated approach, developed over the past 20 years by Phillip Strain, Samuel Odem, Howard Goldstein, and their associates, typical peers are taught to repeatedly initiate "play organizers" such as sharing, helping, giving affection, and praise." Other studies (Hoyson et al., 1984; Strain et al., 1979; Strain et al., 1977; Goldstein et al., 1992) noted the power of these peer mediated strategies to increase not only social interaction, but maintenance and generalization of the social skills at the preschool level. Oke and Schreibman (1990) and McGee and colleagues (1992) expanded upon past studies and found similar positive results when typical peers were trained to promote appropriate social interaction in children with Autism. These approaches have been assembled by Danko et al., 1998 into a manual and have also been described in other publications.

An additional point of interest revealed in the research is that "interactions established between children with Autism and adults do not easily generalize to peer partners" (Bartak and Rutter, 1973). Given this information, it is important to take an intentional step in a general education classroom to, at the very least, begin a foundation for the development of a relationship between the typical peers and the students with an Autism Spectrum Disorder or other disability, which is based on a shared understanding.

The purpose of this manual is to meet the need of professionals to provide trained human resources to students with ASD by implementing a structured procedure that can help both professionals and parents begin the learning and awareness process for typical peers.

Historically similar activities were called "Disability Awareness". The activities might focus on one specific disability group or on several types of disabilities. Some of the activities involved puppets, videos or simulation activities.

This style of activity creates a general awareness of the characteristic of a disability, but often lacks information that could provide a foundation for a friendship and individual support.

This manual differs from disability awareness because it begins by focusing on abilities and friendships, not the disability. To move to the level of friendship, information needs to be shared in a different way. Friendship is based on a shared history, likes, dislikes, and proximity. Friendships typically last over a period of time and are characterized by a preference to be together while engaging in reciprocal, helpful, and positive interactions.

Unfortunately, when a student with a disability enters a general education classroom many of the characteristics of a friendship may be missing. Oftentimes, there is not a shared history because students with ASD may not start at the beginning of the year; or they may not be attending their neighborhood school. These situations require the teachers, school staff, and parents to come together to develop a plan that will foster friendships. This manual provides a simple planning form to gather basic information for the activity. The basic steps for implementing the awareness activity are described. Variations on the ability awareness theme are presented to provide ideas for various age groups, as well as, ideas for introducing information about the student's disability. Case studies give the reader real life examples of how the activities have proven to develop support and friendship for a student with ASD. This manual also offers the reader an extensive list of resources including books for every age group, along with books to assist the student with ASD in developing a self awareness.

This manual may be used as a general guideline or a facilitator may follow the steps as they are specifically outlined. The reader is reminded that ability awareness is not a once a year activity. The resources provide additional ideas for on-going understanding of ASD and relationships. The ultimate goal of using this manual is to provide professionals and parents with tools to help them develop a plan that will lead to a support network of peers, which the research indicates promotes better opportunities for social success for the student with an
Autism Spectrum Disorder or other disability.

What Makes School Great?
PLANNING CHECKLIST

Section 1: Basic Information

Student:	Grade:	School:
Date of Activity:	Time:	Length:
Parent:	Phone:	
Parent Permission Granted: YES ☐; NO ☐	Date:	By:
Teacher:	Phone:	
Other:		

Section 2: Purpose and Participation

Expected Outcome:	Comment:
General Knowledge: ☐ Specific Knowledge: ☐ Other: ☐	Describe:
Parent Participation: YES ☐; NO ☐ If YES, How? Attend: ☐ Other: ☐	Describe:
Student Participation: YES ☐; NO ☐ If YES, How? Attend: ☐ Other: ☐	Describe:

Section 3: Student Information for Shared Understanding

Likes and Interests	Strengths	Things that are hard

Table 1.1

CHAPTER 1:
GETTING STARTED

What Makes School Great? FRIENDS! is an ability awareness activity designed to develop a shared knowledge of common interests and a foundation for friendship, common understanding, and support for a peer with an Autism Spectrum Disorder (ASD) or other disability. The activity may be facilitated by any school staff member (general or special educator, speech pathologist, school psychologist, program specialist, administrator, or para-educator) who feels comfortable leading a group of students through the steps.

To implement an awareness activity the facilitator will need to do some planning and preparation. The *Planning Checklist (see Table 1.1)* provides the facilitator a tool to gather information that is necessary to implement an ability awareness activity. A completed sample *Planning Checklist* (see Table 1.5) is at the end of this chapter.

To assist the facilitator preparing for the activity a reproducible copy of the checklist is provided as a fold out on the last page of this manual. Permission to copy this checklist for noncommercial educational purposes is granted to any facilitator using this manual.

The checklist is divided into three sections which cover Basic Information *(see Table 1.2)*, Purpose and

Participation *(see Table 1.3)*, and Student Information for Shared Understanding *(see Table 1.4)*.

The following instructions will assist the facilitator complete each section of the *Planning Checklist*.

Basic Information

Section 1: Basic Information				
Student		Grade		School
Date of Activity		Time		Length
Parent			Phone	
Parent Permission Granted: YES ☐; NO ☐		Date		By
Teacher			Phone	
Other				

Table 1.2

Section 1

This section provides a place to keep all pertinent basic information regarding the activity. The grade level of the class is very important information as it will help determine the type of presentation and the length of time that will be spent with the group. The younger the age group, the shorter the length of the presentation. Some schools may request that several classes, at a specific grade level, be included in a single presentation; or they may want to provide the information for all primary or intermediate classes. Large group awareness activities can be successfully presented; however, when the goal is to develop personal relationships more student participation is required, which is difficult in a very large group. To facilitate more personal interaction and begin to build shared knowledge, it is recommended that no more than two classes come together for an activity. If time permits, it is always preferable to address one classroom at a time.

It is important to have the contact information for the parent and the classroom teacher, or lead teacher if several classes will be addressed at one time. Parents should be informed of any type of awareness activity. This is important because whether the activity is on a general topic (such as friendship) or a disability specific topic (such as ASD) it will have a direct impact on their child's skills within the classroom. This is especially true for students with ASD who experience a core deficit in the area of socialization and relationships. If it is a disability specific activity, and the child is not going to be singled out, the parent should be informed and requested to give permission to proceed with the activity.

The very youngest student recognizes differences in others. Doing a disability specific activity a facilitator may inadvertently draw attention to the student with the disability, thus starting questions that possibly neither the professional nor parent are ready to respond to. The request for permission is also an invitation for participation.

Purpose and Participation

Section 2: Purpose and Participation	
Expected Outcome:	Comment:
General Knowledge: ☐ Specific Knowledge: ☐ Other: ☐	Describe:
Parent Participation: YES ☐; NO ☐ If YES, How? Attend: ☐ Other: ☐	Describe:
Student Participation: YES ☐; NO ☐ If YES, How? Attend: ☐ Other: ☐	Describe:

Table 1.3

Section 2

Purpose and Participation: The expected outcome and type of participation by the parent and student with ASD or other disability may be simply outlined in this section. There should always be a discussion to determine the general purpose and expected outcome of the activity with the general educator and parent either together or separately. As mentioned before, an awareness activity is more than just a one-time event. Ability awareness must become an on-going growth process that begins with one event.

General Knowledge: The *General Knowledge* box should be checked if the activity is to present any general information such as friendship, similarities and differences, teasing, bullying, or meeting someone new. The box to the right should be used to briefly describe the desired outcome.

Specific Knowledge: The *Specific Knowledge* box should be checked when either a specific disability or disabilities are going to be presented. This box should also be checked if a specific child is going to be discussed whether or not his/her disability will be disclosed. If the specific disability is going to be discussed it is extremely important for the facilitator to know, prior to the activity, the degree to which the specific child understands his/her own disability. Depending on the level of understanding and age of the student it might be important to get his/her permission as well. The right to confidentiality prevails in all specific awareness activities. Thus, even if it appears that it would be helpful for peers to understand why a student with a disability relates to others in a different way, it is imperative that if parents and/or student do not want to share personal information, that their wishes are respected. When a family is hesitant to share personal information the facilitator should only provide a general awareness activity. The space on the right can be used to note comments on participation.

Parent Participation: Parents of the focus student should always have the option of attending and participating in the awareness activities whether the activity is general or specific in nature. Depending on the type of activity, some focus student parents may want to attend as an observer to gain the knowledge of what their child and the classmates are learning. Other parents may only feel comfortable verbally providing background information needed in Section 3 *(see Table 1.4)* prior to the specific activity. Some parents have created photo collages and small story books about their child to be shared with classmates. Occasionally, parents have volunteered to bring a special treat for the class after the activity. Parents who feel comfortable speaking in the class may choose to participate as a contributor from the audience or as the leader of an activity to share things like family history, dreams, likes, strengths, dislikes, and areas in which their child may require help. Regardless of the level of parent participation, collaboration with the parent is vital to the success of awareness activities. Parent participation has been observed to have a powerful impact on both student and professional participants. It is a very visual and concrete way to show general education students that the student with disabilities is more like them than different from them. Meeting the parent of any classmate contributes to a shared history and understanding.

Student Participation: The decision to include the focus student in either a general or specific awareness activity is dependent on several variables. The first variable is the preference of the parents. Parents know their child and should make this decision. Professionals may share their opinions as to the pros and cons of a student's participation, but the final decision should be the parents.

A few reasons to include the student with disabilities in an awareness activity include, but are not limited to the following:

- The activity is general and may help the student learn foundational friendship skills.
- The activities are planned to form peer groups based on interests.
- If the activity is incorporated into a "Student or Star of the Week" program and the student may enjoy the individual attention.
- The student has requested awareness activities to help his/her peers understand ASD and how friendship may be difficult. These requests have been made by students as young as first grade and up through high school. The average age for a student to request this activity is fourth to eight grade.

A few reasons NOT to include the focus student in

an awareness activity include, but are not limited to the following:

- The student's attention span and ability to participate would prevent successful participation.
- The student has no awareness of his disability and might be confused by a specific discussion.
- There are specific problematic behaviors that need to be addressed which might make both the student with disabilities and other students uncomfortable.
- The student with disabilities does not want to participate.

Student Information for Shared Interest

Section 3: Student Information for Shared Understanding		
Likes and Interests	Strengths	Things that are hard

Table 1.4

Section 3

This section *(see Table 1.4)*, of the *Planning Checklist* is provided for the facilitator to gather, prior to the activity, personal information about the student with ASD or other disabilities. This information can be used in either general or student specific awareness activities.

Likes and Interests: Identifying likes and interests is very important because common interests and preferences are part of the foundation for building a friendship. This information can be used in a general friendship building activities without identifying the student by:
- Covertly assisting the student with ASD to join others that have similar interests.
- Using the likes and interests of the student with ASD as the basis for forming activity groups.

This information can be used in specific awareness activities by:
- Listing the likes and interests and asking for a show of hands to indicate who likes the same thing. Next the facilitator may introduce the student with disabilities as a peer who likes all the things listed.
- Using the list to develop related interests.
- Using the list to identify new knowledge about a peer.

Strengths: It is important to recognize that everyone has strengths even if they have a disability. Strengths can be used to develop friendships. When asked, "What a friend might do?" a common response given by a typical child is to say, "My friend helps me sometimes."

Information on a student's strengths can be used in a general friendship building activity without identifying the student by:

- Identifying the strength and soliciting ideas about how a person with that strength could be a helpful friend.
- Using the strengths of a student with ASD as the basis for forming activity groups who could plan how they might help others who don't share the same strength.

This information can be used in specific awareness activities by:

- Asking the student to identify his/her strength (what he/she is good at) and what these strengths help him/her do.
- Having typical peers identify what the student with ASD is good at and share how that strength could help them.

Things That Are Hard. Although the things that are hard for the student with ASD oftentimes are the reasons that an awareness activity is planned, the difficulties should not be the whole focus of any awareness activity. Every person has things that are more difficult for them. Recognizing that everyone needs help on the things that are difficult is part of awareness activities and friendship. As the children always say, "My friends help me." It is learning to give and receive the help that may be the challenge for the student with disabilities, as well as other students.

Information about what is hard for a student can be used in a general friendship building activities without identifying the student by:

- Covertly identifying what is hard and soliciting ideas about how a friend could help that person.
- Using the things that are hard for the student with ASD as the basis for forming peer support groups who could work together on similar issues.

This information can be used in specific awareness activities by:

- Asking the student to identify things that are hard for him to do and what helps him.
- Having typical peers identify what they think is difficult and how they could be a helpful friend.

A completed sample *Planning Checklist* (see Table 1.5) concludes this chapter. The sample *Planning Checklist* below has been completed using anonymous names and locations. (Any similarity to real persons or locations is purely coincidental.)

What Makes School Great? PLANNING CHECKLIST

Section 1: Basic Information

Student: **Fred Jones**	Grade: **3rd**	School: **Ross Elementary**
Date of Activity: **09-10-07**	Time: **10:15**	Length: **45 min.**
Parent: **Fay Jones**	Phone: **000-111-2222**	
Parent Permission Granted: YES ☑; NO ☐	Date: **09-03-07**	By: **Program Specialist**
Teacher: **Mrs. Day**	Phone: **000-222-3333**	
Other: **Mr. Sims, Principal**		

Section 2: Purpose and Participation

Expected Outcome:	Comment:
General Knowledge: ☐ **Fred is new** Specific Knowledge: ☑ **to Ross Elem.** Other: ☐ **Parents want peers to understand him.**	Describe: **Fred wants to have friends, but has difficulty making friends due to his lack of social understanding.**
Parent Participation: YES☑; NO ☐ If YES, How? 　　　　Attend: ☑ Other: ☑	Describe: **Mom will bring pictures of Fred's family and a small treat for after the activity**
Student Participation: YES ☑; NO ☐ If YES, How? 　　　　Attend: ☑ Other: ☑	Describe: **Fred knows he has Autism, but it does not bother him. He will answer questions about Section 3.**

Section 3: Student Information for Shared Understanding

Likes and Interests	Strengths	Things that are hard
~ *Disney movies* ~ *Reading* ~ *Drawing* ~ *Playing the piano*	~ *Good Reader* ~ *Great speller* ~ *Happy most of the time* ~ *Wants to do a good job*	~ *Math* ~ *Playing at recess* ~ *Knowing the rules* ~ *Thinking about other's interests*

Table 1.5

CHAPTER 2:
BASIC STEPS FOR AWARENESS ACTIVITY

What Makes School Great? FRIENDS!

Introducing a Student with Disabilities to a General Education Classroom. The following seven steps are designed to cover the topics of friendship, how to be a friend, and what friends share. This awareness activity may be implemented as presented or with any number of variations based on the expected outcomes as identified on the *Planning Checklist (see Table 1.1)* or the age of the group. This format has been successfully used in classes from kindergarten through high school with the modifications to make each step appropriate to the age group.

The outcome of this specific *What Makes School Great? FRIENDS!* activity is to introduce the student with disabilities, who, for the purpose of this training manual, will be called "focus student" when compared to his general education peers. The focus student could be a student who spends all or part of his day in the general education setting.

Step 1: Identifying Feelings before School Starts. Ask the students to think back to the night before the first day of school and share their feelings. Have the adults in the audience share their feelings, too.

> *Facilitator Options*:
> - For younger children the facilitator can capture interest by pretending to give everyone a new thinking cap from a magic box. The students may be instructed to adjust their cap or even describe their new "thinking caps" before asking to recall their feelings.
> - A simple face may be drawn on the board to provide a visual reference to their feelings.
> - Their feelings may be written on the board.
> - Ask for a show of hands to determine how many students shared the same feelings.
>
> *Participant Responses:*
> - These responses usually range from happy and excited to nervous or scared.
> - Students may have more than one emotion to share.

Step 2: Identifying What Makes School Great. Ask the students and staff to share what made them feel great once they got to school on the first day. The purpose of this guided question is to arrive at the conclusion that friends, old or new, are what makes school great. This response is typical whether one is feeling uncomfortable or comfortable on the first day of school. This response will be the topic starter for Step 3.

Facilitator Options:
- Draw a picture to provide a visual reference of comments.
- Write what made the students feel great on the board.
- Take a vote or ask for a show of hands to confirm that all agree the number one thing that made school great for them was being with friends; then move on to the next step.

Participant Responses:
- There will be a variety of responses; however, within the first five responses a student will typically comment that having friends, or seeing old friends, or making new friends is "what makes school great."

Step 3: Identifying Elements of Friendship. Ask the students and staff to name one thing they like to do with friends or what being a friend means. Adjust the question to the age of the group. Listen for activities that have been identified by the focus student so that the activities preferred by the focus student may be integrated into Step 4.

Facilitator Options:
- Draw a picture to provide a visual reference.
- Write their thoughts on the board.
- Take a vote on agreement of each idea as it is shared.
- A vote may be taken to select the top three ideas about what being a friend means.

Participant Responses:
- Young students may name more activities such as play ball, play tag etc. If this is the case then the facilitator might add the concepts of sharing, helping, taking turns and thinking more about their friend than themselves.

Step 4: Identifying Who Shares the Same Interests with the Focus Student. Using the list of the focus student's favorite items ask the class, "Who would like a friend who likes -----?" (List the items that are preferred by the focus student.)

Facilitators Option:
- Write or draw the focus student's preferences on the board.
- The names of the students who share the same preference may be written beside the list of the focus student's preferences, or note when 100% if the entire class shares the preference.

BASIC STEPS FOR AWARENESS ACTIVITY

Participants Responses:
- There are usually many hands raised for each item and frequently the entire class shares the preference.
- The participants enthusiasm is typically growing at this point.

Step 5: Introducing the New Student. After it is determined that most of the participants would like a friend who likes all the things that were listed, the facilitator announces to them, "It is your lucky day because there is a student in this class (or grade) that likes all those things, too." Then the focus student is introduced. The facilitator explains how the focus student was a little nervous to come to this new class, but now is excited to have classmates to share with some of his or her favorite things.

Facilitators Option:
- If the focus student is present and capable of commenting on his/her interests the facilitator may ask for more details or open it up to the class.
- If the focus student's parent is in the audience they may add additional information.
- If the focus student is not present, but will be joining the class later the peers may be prompted to develop ways to incorporate the new classmates interest into the day and make school great for everyone.

Participants Responses:
- The participants typically all have a positive attitude about meeting a new person with whom they share interests.
- There will be some participants who will immediately show an interest in pursing a relationship and others who will not. Both responses are appropriate and should be respected. With younger participant a larger number of students want to form a friendship. As children age and strong relationships are developed they may be less likely to add a new person to their friendship group.

Step 6: Develop a Plan for Expanding the Friendship with the New Student. Further explore the shared interest with the students. Following this discussion make a plan for the shared interests to grow within the class, on the playground, or at home If the student is present, include him/her as appropriate.

Facilitators Option:
- List the student's ideas to strengthen friendship with the new student and other students in the class.
- Develop an action plan to implement the ideas listed.

- Put the action plan in writing as appropriate to the age group.
- Identify students who would like to help. This step may be left as a classroom follow-up assignment.

Participant Responses:

- Acknowledge what is typical for the age group. Based on the type of response this step may be completed with a small group of interested students at a different time.

Step 7: Recognize All Participants. Congratulate the students for their wonderful ideas about friendship and their participation in welcoming a new student to their class. End the activity with a small treat. If this treat is provided by the parent, then the focus student may choose peers to help distribute the treat.

NOTES & IDEAS FOR APPLICATION:

CHAPTER 3:
VARIATIONS OF AWARENESS ACTIVITIES

Preschool: Awareness activities for the preschooler requires careful consideration of their maturity level, the size of the group, and their attention span. The pre-school child presents differently at each age level between three and five years. For this age group the development of shared interests is the primary focus for awareness activities. Steps 4 -7, outlined in Chapter 3, would be appropriate for this group. Awareness for this age group is accomplished with little steps either in small groups or in larger group activities. Other topics might include similarities and differences, things friends do together, likes and dislikes, and how a friend can be a helper. Developmentally all children in this age group are just learning and refining social relationship skills; thus, learning to share, take turns and thinking about another person, which requires direct instruction for a child with ASD, is part of the curriculum for the typically developing child. Incidental and experiential awareness activities are often most effective with this age group as describe in the following example.

> Mario is four years old and attends a Cooperative Preschool three days a week. At two years of age

he was diagnosed with Autistic Disorder. In spite of intensive intervention Mario had not developed spoken language. He is responsive to a picture exchange system. Although the children at the preschool are nice to Mario there is little to no reciprocal interaction due, in part, to his lack of spoken language. One day during snack Mario was working with a Para professional using his communication book to request his snack items. A curious student asked why Mario could not talk. The student was told that Mario hadn't learned how to talk yet, so he used pictures instead. In a few minutes the peer was taught how to communicate with Mario. This activity resulted in more social exchanges as all the other children wanted to learn how to talk with Mario using pictures.

Kindergarten: The kindergarten age group is more able to participate in a formal lesson as they are beginning to demonstrate a greater understanding of perspective. The activity still must be kept short. The teacher may provide follow-up activities which are incorporated into the curriculum, such as doing a bar graph of all the students likes as identified in Step 4. To sustain the student's attention visualization activities may be incorporated. For instance as mentioned in Step 1, each student is given an imaginary present of a new thinking cap. The facilitator pretends to pass out gift boxes. When each student and staff has a gift box the facilitator pretends to open her box and bring out the thinking cap. Everyone puts his or her thinking cap on, adjust the cap, and then the lesson begins. It is often helpful with this age group to have the focus student's mother and/or father participate in the presentation. The parents may bring baby pictures and family pictures which provides the beginning of a shared history. The following example demonstrates how a mother helped the facilitator introduce her son to his new kindergarten classmates.

> Chuck was going to start kindergarten at his neighborhood school. Now, he was going to be going to school with his siblings. Everyone was excited, but also a little apprehensive since Chuck has Autism and had not attended a general education classroom on a full-time basis. He had been participating in early intervention programs at home and in special classes since he was diagnosed at age two years. He had developed some language readiness skills and play skills; however, his restricted patterns of behavior and sensory issues occasionally caused him to behave in unusual ways. To help his new classmates understand Chuck a little better his Mom wrote a book called, I'm A Lot Like You! (see Appendix A). In this book she talked about his family, his likes, what was hard for him, what he did when he was

upset, and how his classmates could be helpful friends. There were many wonderful pictures that illustrated how Chuck and his peers were more alike than different. Chuck had a good year in kindergarten and still attends his neighborhood school with friends who understand him.

1st and 2nd Grades: If the student with disabilities has been attending the same school with basically the same group of students the facilitator may opt to omit Steps 1 and 2 from the *What Makes School Great? FRIENDS!* activity. The activity could begin by with Step 3 and a focus on friendship. Students in this age group can participate in activities that last a little longer.

Based on the expected outcomes the facilitator might try a different introductory activity. The introduction might focus on similarities and differences. The activity could begin by identifying things that an individual is born with, such as eye color or hair color. This could be compared to things that are acquired, such as likes and dislikes. Step 3 can then expand to cover accepting individual difference.

With this age group, books on friendship might also be incorporated into the activity either as an introduction or as a follow-up by the classroom teacher. There are many books listed for this and other age groups in the

VARIATIONS OF AWARENESS ACTIVITIES

Resources on Ability Awareness section at the end of this manual. The following example describes how, after reading a book, the children were led in an activity to write their own book *(see Appendix B)*.

> Molly attends first grade at her neighborhood school. She had been diagnosed with High Functioning Autism in preschool. She has good verbal skills, is an excellent decoder and has great rote memory for facts. Her restricted patterns of behavior and resistance to change cause her a great deal of difficulty interacting with her peers. She wants to have friends but is often too assertive and demanding, thus causing her peers to stay away from her. Molly's parents felt that her classmates needed to understand the underlying reasons for Molly's behavior and gave permission for her disability of Autism to be presented. They did not think that Molly was ready for this type of presentation so they kept her home the morning of the presentation. Beverly Bishop's book, My Friend with Autism, was used to introduce the activity. This book focuses on things that are easy for children with Autism and things that are difficult. The book concludes by suggesting ways children with Autism can be helped.
> After reading this book the children identified Molly's strength, what was hard for her, and finally what they could do as friends to help her.

The student's ideas were listed on the board. They were then given a three page booklet to write a story about Molly. They started the story with her strength, then added what her Autism made hard for her, and finally what they were going to do to help her (see Appendix B). They illustrated their pages and shared them with the facilitator on a return visit. This and other on-going awareness activities have helped Molly and her classmates grow. Molly continues to attend her neighborhood school and make improvements in all areas.

3rd – 5th Grades (Disability Specific): If the student is new to the school all steps may be followed until Step 5. At Step 5 the idea that certain things are difficult for the focus student may be introduced. The students may be asked to identify what they have observed. The disability may be described without actually naming it, or the disability may be named. If the disability is named it should be done in a neutral manner explaining that this is just the way the focus student was born. The comparison of being born with specific eye and hair color can be made. If the focus student is present he or she may want to make a comment. It is important to point out that the disability is not contagious. Follow-up activities may include reading disability specific books or watching DVDs that explain the disability. (*See Resources for specific titles.*)

VARIATIONS OF AWARENESS ACTIVITIES

General educators may also want to infuse the awareness into writing assignments, art, P.E., literature, and social studies.

If the student has been attending the same school for many years and his or her disability has been named, the steps many be altered to meet the current learning needs of the class. The class may start at Step 4 and identify the strengths, interests, and what is hard for the focus student that they have observed. A disability specific book may be read. A follow-up activity for the upper grades might be to write their own awareness book specific to the focus student they know or develop plans for how they can help the focus student improve in the areas that are difficult for him/her. The following example is from a third grade classroom.

> Wes is a third grade student who had been attending the same school since kindergarten. Although Wes has many skills, his inability to self-regulate his emotional responses in a general education setting prevented him from full time placement in general education. When the school staff was preparing to begin to include Wes more in the general education classroom, the team decided that awareness activities were necessary for the typical peers. Because Wes had been attending a Special Day Classroom the team (including the parents) decided that it was important for his classmates to understand Autism and how this

affected Wes' behavior, learning, communication, and social responses. His third grade teacher decided to follow up after the awareness activity with an expository writing assignment for his class. His third grade class developed the following essay with each student creating an illustration to represent the focus student in class.

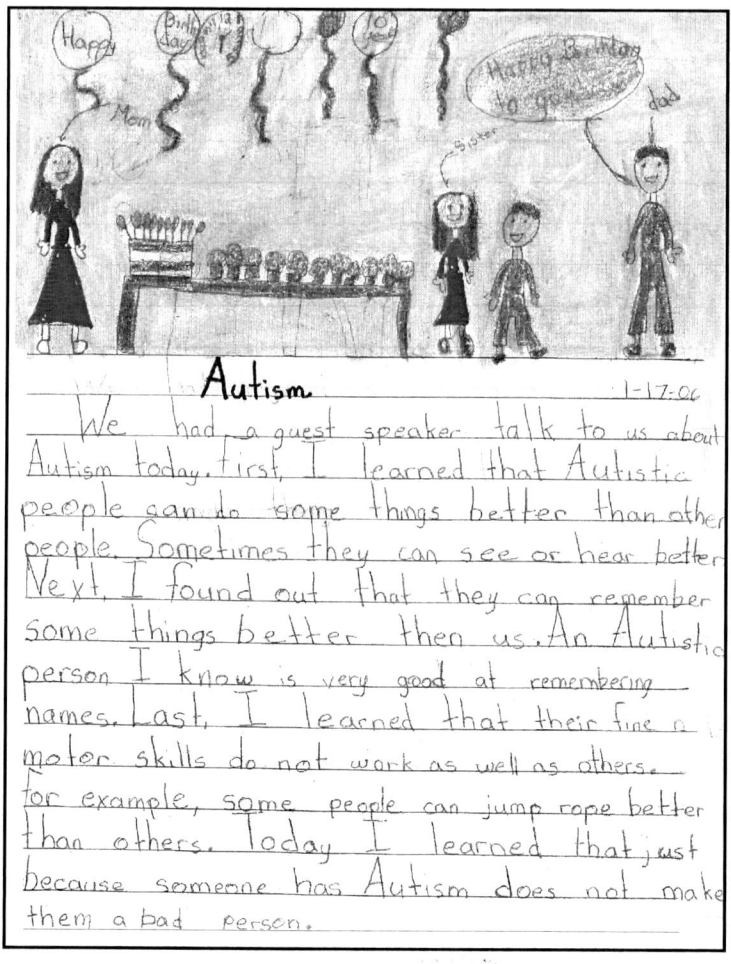

Autism   1-17-06

We had a guest speaker talk to us about Autism today. First, I learned that Autistic people can do some things better than other people. Sometimes they can see or hear better. Next, I found out that they can remember some things better then us. An Autistic person I know is very good at remembering names. Last, I learned that their fine motor skills do not work as well as others. For example, some people can jump rope better than others. Today I learned that just because someone has Autism does not make them a bad person.

VARIATIONS OF AWARENESS ACTIVITIES

6th – 12th Grades: Students in these grades are usually able to take a more in-depth look at what makes school great for themselves and others. If there is a need to introduce a new student to a school, all the steps may be followed at a sophistication level appropriate to the grade. Activities such as *The Sixth Sense* by Carol Gray may be added in place of Steps 1 and 2, to assist the students in developing a better understanding of the causes of the social difficulties experienced, especially by students with an Autism Spectrum Disorder or other social cognitive disabilities. More detailed characteristic of the specific disability may be shared. When discussing Autism Spectrum Disorders, the group may be taught the three core deficit areas of socialization, communication, and restricted patterns of behavior. The class may be able to identify the focus student's strengths and difficulties under the three areas, thus giving the class a more specific picture of how the disability affects the focus student. These older age groups often will develop specific plans for friendship and supports for the current year or for the future. They may also identify growth they have seen over time. This example describes participation at the high school level.

> Jacob was diagnosed with High Functioning Autism in preschool. He entered his neighborhood school in kindergarten. He spent his entire school career in the same school district transitioning through the

grades with the same peers. Upon entering a high school, which drew from many districts, his IEP team decided that these new peers should develop an understanding of Autism and how it affected Jacob's learning and ability to interact socially. Jacob knew he had Autism but he did not dwell on this. He had other things to do like read the dictionary or the encyclopedia and pursue his interest in facts. When Jacob was ask if he would like to participate in a few Autism Awareness activities in his classes he declined saying, "I already know about Autism, I would like to go and read."

In the beginning of Jacob's freshman, sophomore, and junior years in high school, awareness activities were held in each of his six classes. Jacob was accepted by his peers and respected for his strengths and supported in his areas of difficulty. In the beginning of Jacob's senior year it was decided that the awareness activities were no longer needed. Although Jacob still required adult assistance in certain areas of academic and social life on campus he was a member of the clubs and appreciated on campus for his strengths.

Discussing Problem Behaviors across the Age Groups:

When the goal of the activity is to discuss problem behaviors it is usually best if the focus student is not present. The peer group usually feels more comfortable identifying their concerns. The activity may start with Step 3. Step 4 may be modified to ask, "What would it be like if your friend is not able to be a friend?" In Step 5, the facilitator might ask if the students or teacher have noticed any problems that the focus student may have. If disability specific information is to be provided, it could be provided at this point. If no specific disability information is to be given, then as the problems are identified the facilitator may ask why they think the student is doing the identified problem behavior and how they think a friend might help the focus student with the particular problems. Strategies that may be provided to add to the student's ideas include:

- Identify the replacement behavior so all the students know the goal.
- Give the typical students specific words to say or actions to take.
- Role play interaction and methods for support.
- Make a list of friendship ideas for the target student to learn.
- Draw a picture of their ideas and make a class book.

- Set up a system of reinforcement for demonstration good friendship skills for all members of the class.
- Create videos or photo album that show great friendship behavior.

Mickey was diagnosed with Asperger Syndrome in third grade. Mickey has a history of uncooperative behavior. Occasionally, he would growl or shake his fist at peers or staff if he was angry. The IEP team felt it was very important to explain to Mickey's peers why his social skills were not typical for his age. *What Makes School Great? FRIENDS!* and *The Sixth Sense* activities where blended and a frank discussion of the problem behaviors and strategies to assist Mickey were discussed with Mickey out of the classroom. Follow up sessions included Mickey and involved activities to help the class identify shared interest so that Mickey and his peers could begin to learn to interact. Small social groups were set up during recess and lunch to facilitate social interaction.

CHAPTER 4:
CASE STUDIES

High Functioning Autism. Evan is a seventh grade student on a middle school campus in the same school district that he has attended since kindergarten. Evan was diagnosed with Autistic Disorder at 24 months of age. Evan's language was delayed, however with speech therapy his verbal skills developed. He appeared to have normal cognition. His greatest areas of difficulty were his extreme rigidity for routines and sensory processing issues. He attended an inclusion preschool class that served students with Individual Educational Plans and typically developing peers. This class was taught by a special educator. Due to his difficult patterns of behavior, when he transitioned to public school, he was placed in a Special Day Class with some mainstreaming into kindergarten. His parents requested a full time placement in a general education classroom for first grade. Although he was ranked number one student in reading decoding in his class, he continued to have significant difficulty with basic student behaviors and with social interactions. Evan required many supports to be successful in the general education setting including additional staff support, environmental, and academic accommodations.

Evan's ability awareness activities began, when he entered his new school at first grade. Evan was no longer attending his neighborhood school and neither the staff or students knew him. Because Evan was being introduced to the campus the first awareness activity was *What Makes School Great? FRIENDS!* Evan was always present during the activities. As a younger student Evan participated on a limited basis and basically was in the class, but not paying much attention unless something caught his interest. Because his patterns of behavior were significantly different from his peers, his classmates were told about Autism and how it affected Evan. Each year variations of *What Makes School Great? FRIENDS!* were presented to his classmates. His peers, now his friends, have been instrumental in making Evan's learning environment the best it can be.

When Evan was in fifth grade he became a more active participant in the back to school awareness activity for two reasons. First, he had learned appropriate student behaviors and social skills from his peers and staff. Second, the activity was presented using a visual tool, the Venn diagram, which Evan used consistently in his school work. This group of fifth grade students acknowledged both Evan's strengths and weaknesses saying, "That's just Evan." The outcome of the fifth grade awareness activity was to focus on the new skills Evan would need when he transitioned with his class to middle school. The class was confident that the transition to middle school would be a success because they would be with him to provide friendship and support as needed. The students were correct and the transition to middle school was a success.

Awareness activities continue to be a part of Evan's school year. The focus now is not on getting to know Evan but more about how to help him meet the ever changing academic and social demands. His friends helped him naturally throughout the day by volunteering their support. There is a weekly "Lunch Bunch" that is comprised of boys and girls who have gone to school with him since elementary school. Evan has his friendship files and loves to hang out with his friends and take their pictures for his scrapbooks.

Awareness activities along with consistent ongoing proximity, shared interests, and a shared history create positive relationships and provide a solid foundation for friendships.

Classic Autistic Disorder/Non-verbal. Frank is currently a fourth grade student who is receiving his primary services in a Special Day Class for students with mild to moderate disabilities. Frank was diagnosed with Autism prior to 36 months of age. He was not verbal. Frank participated in an intensive home program and at the age of four years he attended a private preschool with a tutor. In both his preschool setting and his kindergarten class, his peers were provided with awareness activities. At the preschool level they were informal and experiential with a focus on teaching the peers to be a communication partner, using Frank's picture communication system. Frank transitioned to his neighborhood school for kindergarten. *What Makes School Great? FRIENDS!* was used with a focus on Frank's use of pictures to communicate. The peers learned the system and provided many opportunities for practice. Frank transitioned to a Special Day Class for first grade. Frank's family wanted to ensure that he had opportunity to interact daily in a meaningful way with typical peers. Again the *What Makes School Great? FRIENDS!* activity was used to establish an understanding of Frank's needs. Frank did not participate in these activities, as the activities did not hold much interest for him. Two of Frank's favorite activities were running and playing with balls. The students were asked to think about Frank's interests and activities and identify something that would be fun for him to do at recess. The students decided on soccer, but then realized that the rules would be too hard for him to learn and that the game moved too fast for him. The group identified running and kicking a ball with a group as something they could teach Frank that would be fun for everyone.

Everyone in the class signed up to be part of Frank's "Fun Friends at Recess" group. There were four groups with five students in each group. The students met Frank and a staff at the beginning of recess and played the modified soccer game that the students developed. At the end of the year the class evaluated Frank's progress and listed all the skills he had learned beside kicking and running. The entire group and Frank were proud of themselves and ready to plan for the next year.

The next year there were two classes that participated in Frank's program. These classes continued the recess skills and asked if Frank could come to their classes for other activities and all the field trips. Although Frank did not participate in academic activities he was definitely a welcomed member of the general education class, with

What Makes School Great? FRIENDS!

a circle of friends who greeted him at school and in the community.

Asperger Syndrome: Clark was diagnosed with hyperlexia in preschool. Clark was very verbal and academically advanced for his age. He had difficulty with social interactions, transitions, and a rigid adherence to routines. It was always assumed that given his high cognitive skills, his other difficulties would correct themselves. The opposite seemed to be true. During the primary grades Clark had difficulty making and keeping friends. He would frequently be disruptive in class. In the fourth grade he was diagnosed with Asperger Syndrome. His parents requested that the diagnosis be kept confidential. When Clark transitioned to middle school he also moved to a new school district.

The school welcomed Clark; however the staff was unfamiliar with the needs of a student with Asperger Syndrome. Clark did not know a single student on campus and his social difficulties were magnified in the eyes of peers who did not understand some of his unconventional responses to social situations. It was decided that everyone on campus needed awareness activities.

Clark's family decided that before other people could learn about how Asperger Syndrome affected Clark, that Clark needed to understand the reason for his social difficulties at school. Therefore, the first awareness activity was with Clark. His parent requested assistance from an Autism Specialist who had worked with Clark in a social skills group and had a rapport with him. During a home visit, Asperger Syndrome was discussed in general as it related to students who had difficulty with social skills. The book *Finding Out about Asperger Syndrome, High Functioning Autism and PDD* (Gerland 1997) was shared with Clark and his family. Clark thought about the information that had been shared and then asked, "Is that why sounds are always so loud in my ears?" From that time on Clark learned as much as he could about Asperger Syndrome.

General awareness activities were held with his classmates as Clark was not ready to disclose that he had Asperger Syndrome. He was comfortable talking with his teachers and shared information with them at his IEP meetings.

He now knew why he had difficulty making friends and was motivated to work actively on friendship skills. One day he said, "Thinking about how to be a friend is exhausting."

Clark is in high school and building friendships around

What Makes School Great? FRIENDS!

shared interests. He has even helped younger children with ASD understand that there are lots of "cool" things you can do when you have ASD and that real friends are "OK" with you just the way you are.

REFERENCES

Bartak, L., and Rutter, M. (1973). Special education treatment of autistic children: A comparative study: I. Design of study and characteristics of units. *Journal of Child Psychology and Psychiatry and Allied Disciplines 14(3):161-178.*

Danko, C.D., Lawry, J. and Strain, P.S. (1998 unpublished) *Social Skills Interventions Manual Packet.* Pittsburg, PA: St. Peters Child Development Center.

Gray, C. (2002) *The Sixth Sense II.* Arlington, TX: Future Horizons, Inc. http://www.FutureHorizons-Autism.com

Gerland, G. (1997) *Finding Out about Asperger Syndrome, High Functioning Autism and PDD.* London, England: Jessica Kingsley Publishers.

Kinny, J. and Fischer, D. (2001) *Co-Teaching Students with Autism K-5.* Verona, WI: IEP Resources. http://www.attainmentcompany.com

National Research Council. (2001) *Educating Children with Autism.* Washington DC: National Academy Press.

Ozonoff, S., Rogers, S., and Hendren, R. (2003) *Autism Spectrum Disorders: A Research for Practitioners.* London, England: American Psychiatric Publishing.

Wolfberg, P. (2003) *Peer Play and the Autism Spectrum.* Shawnee Mission, KS: Autism Aspergers Publishing Company. http://www.asperger.net

RESOURCES ON ABILITY AWARENESS

Ability Awareness Books for Young to Elementary Age Children

Bishop, B. (2002) *My Friend with Autism.* Arlington, TX: Future Horizons, Inc. http://www.FutureHorizons-Autism.com

Elder, J. (2006) *Different Like Me: My Book of Autism Heroes.* London, England: Jessica Kingsley Publishing. http://www.jkp.com

Katz, I. and Ritvo, E. (1993) *Joey and Sam.* Northridge CA: Real Life Story Books.

Larson, E. M. (2006) *I Am Utterly Unique: Celebrating the Strengths of Children with Asperger Syndrome and High Functioning Autism.* Shawnee Mission, KS: Autism Aspergers Publishing Company. http://www.asperger.net

Lear, L. (1998) *Ian's Walk: A Story about Autism.* Morton Grove, Illinois: Albert Whitman & Company.

Lowell, J. and Tuchel, T. (2005) *My Best Friend Will.* Shawnee Mission, KS: Autism Aspergers Publishing Company. http://www.asperger.net

Luchsinger, D. and Olson, J. (2007) *Playing by the Rules: A Story about Autism.* Bethesda, MD: Woodbine House.

Maguire, A. (2000) *Special People Special Ways.* Arlington, TX: Future Horizons Inc. http://www.FutureHorizons-Autism.com

Messner, Abby W. (1996) *Captain Tommy.* Arlington, TX: Future Horizons, Inc. http://www.FutureHorizons-Autism.com

Murrell, Diane. (2002) *Tobin Makes Friends.* Arlington, TX: Future Horizons, Inc. http://www.FutureHorizons-Autism.com

Sabin, E. (2006) *The Autism Acceptance Book.* Watering Can Press. http://www.wateringcanpress.com

Simmons, K. (2000) *Little Rainman: Autism through the Eyes of a Child*. Arlington, TX: Future Horizons, Inc. http://www.FutureHorizons-Autism.com

Thompson, M. (1996) *Andy and his Yellow Frisbee*. Bethesda, MD: Woodbine *House.*

Twachtman-Cullen, D. (1998) *Trevor Trevor*. Higganum, CT: Starfish Press. http://www.starfishpress.com

Books for Upper Elementary to Adolescences

Gagnon, E. & Smith-Myles, B. (1999*) This is Asperger Syndrome. London, England: Jessica Kingsley Publishers.*

Hall, K. (2001) *Asperger Syndrome: The Universe and Everything. London, England: Jessica Kingsley Publishers.*

Hoopman, K. (2000) *Blue Bottle Mystery: An Asperger Adventure*. London, England: Jessica Kingsley Publishers. http://www.jkp.com

Hoopman, K. (2001) *Lace and the Lacemaker: An Asperger Adventure.* London, England: Jessica Kingsley Publishers. http://www.jkp.com

Hoopman, K. (2002) *Blue Bottle Mystery: An Asperger Adventure*. London, England: Jessica Kingsley Publishers. http://www.jkp.com

Jackson, L. (2002) *Freaks, Geeks & Asperger Syndrome: A User Guide to Adolescence.* London, England: Jessica Kingsley Publishing. http://www.jkp.com

Keating-Velasco, J.L. (2007) *A is for Autism, F is for Friend*. Shawnee Mission, KS: Autism Aspergers Publishing Company. http://www.asperger.net

Lord, C. (2006) *Rules*. New York, NY: Scholastic.

Orgaz, N. (2002) *Buster and the Amazing Daisy: Adventures with Asperger Syndrome.* Washington DC and London, England: Jessica Kingsley Publishers. http://www.jkp.com

Schnurr, R. (1999) *Asperger's Huh?* Arlington, TX: Future Horizons, Inc. http://www.FutureHorizons-Autism.com

Welton, J. (2004) *Can I tell you about Asperger Syndrome?* A guide for friends and family. Washington DC and London, England: Jessica Kingsley Publishers. http://www.jkp.com

Books for Adults

Attwood, T. (1993*) Why does Chris do that?* Shawnee Mission, KS: Autism Aspergers Publishing Company. http://www.asperger.net

Burrows, E. L. and Wagner, S. J. (2004) *Understanding Asperger's Syndrome, Fast Facts: A Guide for Teachers and Educators to Address the Needs of the Student.* Arlington, TX: Future Horizons, Inc. http://www.FutureHorizons-Autism.com

Grandin, T. (1986) *Emergence Labeled Autistic.* Navato, CA: Warner Books.

Grandin, T. (1996) *Thinking in Pictures and Other Reports from my Life with Autism.* New York, NY: Vintage Books.

Holliday Willey, L. (1999) *Pretending to be Normal.* Washington DC and London, England: Jessica Kingsley Publishers. http://www.jkp.com

Holliday Willey, L. (2001) *Asperger's in the Family: Redefining Normal.* London, England: Jessica Kingsley Publishers, http://www.jkp.com

Ledgin, N. (2002) *Asperger's and Self-Esteem: Insight and Hope Through Famous Role Models.* Arlington, TX: Future Horizons, Inc. http://www.FutureHorizons-Autism.com

Newport, J. (2001) *Your Life is Not a Label: A Guide to Living Fully with Autism and Asperger Syndrome.* Arlington, TX: Future Horizons, Inc. http://www.FutureHorizons-Autism.com

Newport, J., Newport, M., and Dodd, J. (2007) *Mozart and the Whale: An Asperger's Love Story.* New York, NY: Simon and Schuster.

Shore, S. (2003) *Beyond the Wall: Personal Experiences with Autism and Asperger Syndrome.* Shawnee Mission, KS: Autism Aspergers Publishing Company. http://www.asperger.net

Williams, D. (1992) *Nobody, Nowhere: The extraordinary autobiography of an autistic*, New York, NY: Times Books.

Williams, D. (1994) *Somebody, Somewhere: Breaking Free from the World of Autism,* New York, NY: Three River Press.

Williams, D. (1996) *Like Color to the Blind: Soul Searching and Soul Finding.* New York, NY: Times Books.

Books for Self-Awareness

Faherty, C. (2000) Asperger's: *What Does It Mean to Me?* Arlington, TX: Future Horizons, Inc. http://www.FutureHorizons-Autism.com

Korin, E.S. (2006) *Asperger Syndrome an Owner's Manual: What You, Your Parents and Your Teachers Needs to Know.* Shawnee Mission, KS: Autism Asperger Publishing Company.

Korin, E.S. (2007) *Asperger Syndrome an Owner's Manual for Older Adolescents and Adults: What You, Your Parents and Friends, and Your Employer, Needs to Know.* Shawnee Mission, KS: Autism Asperger Publishing Company.

WEBSITES

The Autism Society of Delaware: This organization is comprisedmembers and friends of people with, and professionals who work in thefield. Their mission is to improve the lives of people with Autism and their families. They educate, advocate and raise public awareness in order to promote lifelong opportunity and acceptance for people with Autism in their communities. The website listed below is for kids only and is designed to help children understand ASD.
http://www.delAutism.org/kids_only.htm

The TEACCH Program: A Division of the Department of Psychiatry mission is to enable individuals with Autism to function as meaningfully and as independently as possible in the community; to provide exemplary services throughout North Carolina to individuals with Autism and their families and those who serve and support them. As a member of the University community, to generate knowledge; to integrate clinical services with relevant theory and research; and to disseminate information about theory, practice, and research on Autism through training and publications locally, nationally and internationally. The following link on their website provide generic and specific awareness activities.
http://www.teacch.com/understandingfriends.html

VIDEO/DVD RESOURCES

Intricate Minds: Understanding Classmates with Asperger Syndrome.
Intricate Minds II: Understanding Elementary School Classmates with Asperger Syndrome

Both available at http://www.coultervideo.com

Appendix A
IDEAS FOR PARENTS OR PROFESSIONALS TO CREATE AND USE A PERSONAL AWARENESS BOOK

I'm A Lot Like You!

This outline may be used as presented or varied to meet the individual needs of the child and the situation. The original book was designed to have one or more paragraphs per page. The book may be read straight through or comments from the class can be solicited as the book is read to them.

Page 1. My name is _____.

Page 2. I am _____ years old.
I live with my _____.
I am going to be in your class very soon.

Page 3. I am just like you in a lot of ways.
Some of my favorite things to eat are _____.
But, I really love _____.

Page 4. We might be alike in other ways too.
I like _____.

Page 5. I also like _____.

Page 6. Sometimes I need extra help to do the things I like. I also need a little more help at school. So, a helper will be with me most of the time.
It is hard to understand when people talk to me because I learn differently than you.

Page 7. If I get frustrated or feel scared or tired, I might scrunch up my face, or play with my hands, or even cry. But, I get really upset if you cry because it makes me so sad I don't know what to do.

Appendix B
IDEAS FOR CHILDREN TO WRITE A BOOK

I Have a Friend with Autism

A follow-up activity for children who have participated in a disability specific awareness activity about a classmate is to write a book. This format was expanded upon to allow older students to do a similar writing activity. The following outline provides the details included on each page of the book.

Cover Page: Title "I Have a Friend With Autism"
Written and illustrated by_____.

Page 1: I have a friend with Autism.
I think that my friend is good at_____.

Page 2: Autism makes some things hard for my friend to do.
I think my friend is good at _____.

Page 3: I can be a helpful friend when I _____.